How to Sell Long Term Care Insurance to Mr. and Mrs. Jones; a Guide from Lead Card to Sale

By

Curt Vahle

authorHOUSE™

1663 LIBERTY DRIVE, SUITE 200
BLOOMINGTON, INDIANA 47403
(800) 839-8640
WWW.AUTHORHOUSE.COM

First published by AuthorHouse 11/03/05

ISBN: 1-4208-9068-9 (sc)

Library of Congress Control Number: 2005908978

Printed in the United States of America
Bloomington, Indiana

This book is printed on acid-free paper.

Dedication

To my wife Judy; my best friend and confidant. Without her this wouldn't have been possible. . .trust me. Get to know Judy, read Proverbs 31.

Acknowledgements

- Jim Perry for the push I needed to get into this business.
- Bill Stockdale for showing me the way in.
- Steve Butterfield for giving me the opportunity and showing me how to dress right and look good.
- Dale Larson and Cameron Truesdell for starting a company that became a giant and industry standard.
- The Church of Praise in Eagletown, IN

Contents

Preface

There is nothing new under the Sun.
Ecclesiastes 1:9

This scripture is appropriate. Everything has been done before and nothing in this guide is new. Sometimes though, there are new ways to look at old things. Have you ever tried to teach something to someone and they could never quite get it? Then months or years later they hear the same thing through someone else and suddenly the light goes on. It happens all the time, especially with our children. We want to scream and say, "That's what I tried to tell you, but you wouldn't listen!"

The truth is, what we have to say just doesn't click with everyone. We just aren't received by everyone. I'm hoping that as you go through this guide, the light will click on and you'll get something out of it. This guide does not contain theory, but true sales experience out in the field. Out where the rubber meets the road. Before we begin though, let me share a little about where I came from and what has helped shaped my thinking.

I grew up in a home with a Father in the insurance business, but more importantly, a Father that taught me important things. For instance, he taught me things like how to shake someone's hand, and how to introduce myself while looking them in the eye. Those two things alone were life changing and put me ahead of so many others.

It's sad, but few people ever master those two simple things. Two simple things that done with confidence can open doors of opportunity. Fathers have neglected teaching their Sons and Daughters the basics, and because of it, they are never able to get ahead in life. The number one problem in business, life, and world affairs is the lack of an ability to communicate.

The greatest gift ever given to me and taught by both my parents was that there is a God and his son is Jesus Christ. Now don't get the wrong idea. I was never what you might think of as "religious." In fact, I rebelled hard against my parents and was happy to be a dope smoking hippie for years. Only after I married and got my life on track did I realize the good things they had put in me.

I started working at age 16 in a grocery store stocking shelves and carrying out groceries. In another store I worked in the meat department, became a meatcutter, and worked as one for 14 years. I learned so much behind the meat counter. I learned that the customer is always right, how to satisfy the customer, and how to communicate and deal with suppliers. That you worked until the job was done, and that it pleased the boss when you put out extra effort.

It was during this time that I began taking notice of the salesmen that would come into our store and what I perceived as "the glamorous life." They always seemed upbeat, well dressed, drove a company car and got to travel. Oh to earn $300 a week and drive a company car, that would be the life!

I was married, had four children, was working 45 hours a week cutting meat and delivering papers seven days a week, all for very little money. My heart was crying out that there had to be more. There was a problem however, and for me it turned out to be a big problem. I didn't possess a college degree. I thought at the time that my experience in the meat business would be enough to get me into that special club of the "meat salesmen." I was wrong.

I soon found out that meat companies were not looking for experienced meat people, but college graduates with a degree in anything. I fought on to no avail applying for meat sales positions everywhere. One time I sent a resume to a particular meat packer with a picture of me in a suit on my knees begging for an interview. I thought that surely someone this outgoing and zealous would have to be considered. Wrong again.

I was very discouraged, but God had other plans. In 1989 my wife and I were in Florida vacationing with our pastor and his wife. We had just arrived and sat down in our favorite restaurant, The Oasis in St. Augustine, when something happened that changed my life forever. I began sharing with him my desire to get into sales. He replied that there was a guy (Bill Stockdale) in the church that sells nursing home insurance for a company called AMEX and that maybe I should give him a call. As they say, the rest is history.

My pastor at the time, Jim Perry, had also instilled good things into me. Like the importance of moving on something and not waiting around for things to happen. That sometimes you've got to go for it. I called Bill that day and arranged for a meeting when we returned to Indiana. I couldn't wait to get home! Once home, I went out on an appointment with Bill. I was all dressed up in a brown polyester suit and had a full beard. He graciously opened up to me the possibilities of selling nursing home insurance. Those were the days before it was even called long term care (LTC) insurance.

There was more good news. It turned out that you didn't need a college degree, only a license. That was a revelation. Bill got me an interview with the boss (Steve Butterfield), who snatched me up quickly. I would later realize that if you *want* to sell insurance, that's enough to qualify you, you're hired!

I went on to learn many things, some of which I will be sharing in the pages to come. The main message throughout this book is that you can do it! If a former butcher can, you can too. My very first year in the business I qualified for the company trip to Tahiti, tasted Dom Perignon champagne for the first time, and learned how to dress sharp (thanks Steve). I realized that there were better things than $300 per week and a company car. In closing I'll quote something an old butcher once told me, "No matter how stupid someone is you can still learn something from them." You're about to read a book by a former butcher, just maybe you can learn something too.

Introduction

With thousands of people turning 65 each day, opportunities abound for the long term care (LTC) salesman. Unfortunately, the truth of how to sell LTC insurance seems hidden. I became aware of this over the past few years as I myself changed focus from that of a full time LTC salesman to one that works with agents.

Having the chance to go to different conventions and seeing the abundance of senior product sales tools in the form of books, tapes, videos, etc., I became aware that many who claim to know something about LTC selling actually know very little. It seemed to me that what many agents have been exposed to are "opinions," not experiential knowledge obtained only by working in the field.

LTC companies spend lot's of money doing what they call marketing, but the actual "know how" of selling long term care insurance is hard to be found. We have been surrounded by motivational speakers with so called great ideas, rather than those who have the real goods on the "how-tos of selling." I speak with agents everyday from all over the country that are thirsty for this kind of knowledge.

I began mulling this over sometime back and wondering why there wasn't some kind of guide available for the agent or company that wants to really learn the nuts and bolts of everyday LTC selling. Agents who hunger to learn from those with real life experience in long term care are sentenced to forking out thousands of dollars to those who lack some actual selling experience with time under their belt.

Don't misunderstand me; there is plenty of helpful information available at your finger tips as to *what* LTC insurance is and the huge problems that face the nation's elderly, but very little on *how to sell* LTC insurance. There are myriads of marketing techniques, but very little in the form of a "real life long term care sales guide." Having been an agent in the field, I felt I had some viable solutions to offer. This has been my motivation. To give those who hunger a few basic but powerful tools and ideas that might make a difference in your life.

I want to be clear. I am not a super salesman. What I share comes from my experience as a slightly above average agent that is better at coaching than playing.

When I started as an absolute green horn in November 1989, the LTC business was a whole different ball game than it is today. Policies were extremely simple and there was no real system in place to teach new agents. I started my career with AMEX Life Assurance Company. This is the company that GE purchased to get into the business. I was with AMEX/ GE for a total of eight and one half years as a captive agent, selling only their policy. During that time there was constant change in every facet of the business; from the polices themselves to the way you sold them. It was a wild time and a fun time.

Compared to today standards, when I began my career in 1989, there was no formal training to speak of. In fact, my training consisted of myself and one other new guy in a small conference room for five days talking and role playing with no real outline to guide us. The regional office manager was our trainer, and he was very busy dealing with all the duties of the office, so he was sporadically in and out and rarely there. Compared to what we expect today it was vastly different.

While working there I met some good agents that were old school. They knew some selling keys that I latched on to that really helped my growth as an agent. Many of the things I learned back then I still use to this day. Hopefully I will pass them on to you. What you will find in these upcoming pages is a compellation of many agents' words, actions, phrases, and experiences that I have taken, seasoned with my personality, and made my own. You will do the same. This is not some slick scheme, but a plan that if worked properly will yield fruit.

It is my belief that to most effectively receive from the information contained herein a classroom approach is best. That is how the book was written, as if I were teaching a class. For the experienced professional who needs a guide to instill into others, this book makes a great outline. It is not complicated, nor is it easy. I would say that it is basic and challenging, filled with truths based in reality.

CHAPTER 1

PRODUCT KNOWLEDGE

Concerning product knowledge; to quote a famous movie mobster, "Forget about it." I know you are thinking, "I have to know about product before I can sell long term care insurance." The question you should be asking is, "How much product knowledge do I need to know before I can sell long term care insurance effectively?" The answer, and this will surprise many of you, is that product knowledge doesn't sell long term care insurance.

Some of you just had a sudden rise in your blood pressure. You think that you can't possibly start selling long term care insurance until you know every facet of the policy. If you are that type of individual, affectionately known as anal retentive, then it's going to be very difficult for you to accept what I say. The truth is that I've seen many people, including myself, get caught in the trap of thinking that if I share my vast knowledge of this product I will win the hearts of the prospects and make a sale. Wrong!

A true Salesman understands what the customer wants and what they are buying…**HIM!** Even though it is true that you have to be the expert and you have to know how these policies work, it is not necessary to know everything to be a great Salesman. As time goes by you will become a knowledgeable expert, but that will come only with time and experience. That alone will shape you into the all knowing Long Term Care (LTC) Insurance Specialist!

Having said that, we want to get started and get through product training before we learn how to actually sell. Some of you are wondering why we are starting on product first after my bold statements in the previous paragraphs. If we didn't start with product now, and I made you wait to the very end, most of you would probably bust. The take home message is this: ◊ Product knowledge is important, but don't be overly concerned feeling that you have to know everything about the long term care policy you are selling in order to be an effective salesman. ◊

Hopefully you have already chosen at least one product that you would like to sell. If you have more than one, that's fine, but use only one for this exercise. The ideal way to cover product knowledge is in a classroom setting or at the very least with one other person. The following takes a classroom approach. Here is the order of events in this chapter:

1. Discuss the cost of long term care.
2. Read the Guide to Medicare.
3. Go over the Medicaid rules for your state.
4. Read the brochure and the outline of coverage.

5. Address all questions pertaining to the product.
6. Read the underwriting guide front to back.
7. Fill out all the paperwork; the application, outline of coverage, receipt, etc. as if you were in the home.

Discuss the cost of long term care:

You need to have a knowledge of the cost of long term care (i.e.: nursing home, home health care, assisted living, adult day care) in your area and around the country. This can easily be researched on the internet. I will include some helpful sites at the end of the book. It is important for you the agent to know this information because you will be designing long term care policies based on the cost of care in a given area. In addition, your clients may plan on retiring to another part of the country, so you need to have a basic knowledge of what costs are in various places.

Read the Guide to Medicare:

It is very important that you the agent understand Medicare and how it pertains to long term care. Be sure to read the Guide to Medicare, highlighting all the areas that show exactly what Medicare will pay for, and under what conditions. You will be amazed. Most people that receive long term care get nothing from Medicare because they are in intermediate care, not skilled care. One of the common beliefs of clients is that Medicare will cover their long term care costs. This is simply not the case. Know the facts!

Read the Medicaid rules for your state:

Again, know the facts! Some people believe that Medicaid is *the* answer for paying for long term care, and it is if you want to spend down your assets. It's important to have facts and information in your head and in writing so you can refute the misinformation and lies that people have heard. At the end of this book is a chapter on helpful sources. In it you will find LTC Connection. Through them you can find Medicaid information specific to your state. You will also see the Corporation for Long-Term Care Certification. Through their course, created by attorney Harley Gordon, you will gain important knowledge on long term care issues such as Medicaid.

Read the brochure and the outline of coverage:

Beginning with the brochure, take turns reading the product out loud a paragraph at a time. Don't stop by asking questions at this time, but make notes on the brochure and outline of coverage themselves. Do not write on anything else because it will only muddle things and increase your anxiety. I want you to focus on the product at hand. Here is a gem of truth: ◊ When the client has a question about a benefit or a feature and you're not sure what the answer is offhand, let the brochure or outline of coverage do the speaking for you. ◊

Don't GUESS but let the product speak to them. The absolute worst thing you could do is guess and be wrong. Many times you'll be in the presence of a real old pro and he will purposely try to trip you up just to see how you will respond to him. There is nothing wrong with saying you don't know but you'll have an answer by the end of the day. He or she will respect that about you much more than if you are trying to be a know it all. Another thing, no matter what you may think about retired folk, they didn't just fall off the turnip cart and they do have all the money.

Address all questions pertaining to the product:

Go over your questions one by one so everybody has complete understanding. Stick to the product at hand, don't get off focus.

Read the underwriting guide front to back:

Do this to familiarize yourself with health conditions and their pronunciations. This is where you can really look good to the customer. It gives you more credibility if you know how to pronounce certain health conditions and the medications associated with those problems. You'll feel like a doctor after a while and be able to carry on a conversation with any well respecting Pharmacist in America.

Fill out all the paperwork:

Finally, let's fill out the application, the outline of coverage, receipt, and any other paperwork your product requires just as if you were in the home filling one out with the client. Use yourself as the applicant for the information and go through this together line by line. This next little gem is very important: ◊ ***WHEN YOU'VE MADE A SALE, NEVER LEAVE THE HOME BEFORE YOU HAVE CHECKED TO MAKE SURE THAT ALL THE PAPER WORK IS FILLED OUT!!*** ◊

You will not want to call them later with more questions or have to schedule a call back because you forgot to get them to sign the application. It makes you look bad and can sometimes give your client a reason to cancel the whole thing when he otherwise wouldn't. You are the professional and you need to act like one. Take your time and do it right the first time. Put them at ease with your professionalism.

CHAPTER 2

WHERE IT ALL BEGINS...THE PHONE

The second chapter is really where it all begins; the phone. If you can master the phone, that is if you can set appointments, <u>you will win</u>. That's right, all you have to do is learn how to set appointments and you win. Here is another gem of truth: ◊ Even the worst Salesman will be successful if he or she consistently sets appointments, even the worst. ◊

I have known successful agents through the years that were either too loud or too quiet or too rude or too geeky and would wonder...how the heck did they do it? Well, it always came down to the fact that they were hard workers, they did not quit when it came to setting appointments. Many will not believe this but it is true, the only thing separating the highly successful agent from those that aren't is the <u>number of appointments</u> they work each and every week, not their ability to smooth talk or hard ball someone.

For some of you the thought of going to some strange person's house and talking about LTC Insurance is a scary thought, maybe petrifying. For those of you that feel that way I have one word, RELAX. Going to the home is the fun part. I want you to think about some elderly person that has been in your life, maybe grandma or grandpa, friend or neighbor. You wouldn't get nervous going to see them would you? Well, for the most part that's who your customers are.

Even though the LTC market is getting younger all the time, there are thousands turning 65 each and every day, and they need LTC insurance now! This generation that we are visiting is a gracious generation that for the most part is rarely impolite and always interesting. I always tell new agents that it's like visiting grandma, nice and easy.

Yes, the appointment is nice and easy so relax. The toughest part…**the phone**. . .this is what separates the men from the boys. This is what causes most to fail. Let's thinks about that last sentence…this is what causes **most to fail**!

The odds of making it are not in your favor. In fact, without a full commitment, you will not make it and will go the way of thousands back into the doldrums of everyday life, time-clock punching or sitting in an office dealing with the daily politics. But…if you are willing to take a leap of faith and not quit or waver, then **you will make it**, but it is vital that you stick to a good sales plan.

One of the things that I try very hard to do is to break everything down into a few simple steps because it really is simple, <u>this is not brain surgery</u>. Have you ever heard the saying, "There is none that hath endurance like one who sells insurance." It's really true. The top agents are not more gifted, top agents are just not afraid, and they don't quit. **It is not about your ability to talk a good game, it's about hanging in there.**

So before we get into the simple truths of setting appointments, take a good look at yourself and decide here and now if you want to do this. If this is not something that you really want to do, then I would not venture any farther. However, if you can commit yourself to one year of hard work, just one year, you will never be the same. The thought of sitting behind a desk will be abhorrent and you will never again... punch a clock. So **let's pretend** for the moment that you're through with your training, and you have returned home and are ready to get started in this new adventure. This is how you get started.

HOW TO SET APPOINTMENTS

The night before:

Gem of truth: ◊ Prepare for your phone time and eliminate distractions. ◊ You are on a mission and nothing can be allowed to get in your way. Without a well organized work setting and a focused mind, you increase the odds of poor production, so the night before you make your calls is the time to prepare.

1. First, get your desk or work area cleaned off and looking really good. Get everything off the desk that might distract you, like bills, newspapers, etc. You do this because the time on the phone is a time where you have to be a dialing machine with nothing distracting you, nothing. Again this is basic but extremely powerful and true. Also, make sure you have a schedule calendar

and a sheet of paper to track your dial to contact to appointment ratio.

2. Next, get your lead cards or phone list in order. Look at the zip codes or area codes and organize them accordingly so as to make your job easier. Don't just start calling without knowing where you are going. It's not smart to intentionally set an appointment on the north side of town, go to a south side appointment, only to then go back to a north side appointment. Now of course **life in sales is not an exact science,** so yes, there will be times when your schedule is screwy. Just try to go about it in an organized way.

3. Make sure the phone is in good working condition. Gem: ◊ Your phone call is the first impression your customers have of you. ◊ If you have a crappy sounding phone, get rid of it! Spend some money on a good phone. Preferably a good head set phone so your hands can be free to write and take notes, and remember the key words; a **good** head set. Give somebody a call and ask them how you sound, it's that important.

4. Make sure that nobody will disturb you tomorrow whether you are at home or at the office. This is your appointment setting time and nothing must deter you. I know when I set appointments I prefer to have nobody around. Some agents are not so picky and don't care who is in the room with them. The main point is that you eliminate what distracts YOU!

5. Get the coffee ready and go to bed.

This is how you prepare for the make or break part of the job, "the phone." You will want to review this again when the training is complete. You will in time come up with your own plan of preparation. Whatever it is, stick to it.

The Phone Script:

Before we get into the actual script that I use, it's important to know that it's not <u>WHAT you say, it's HOW you say it</u>. I am sure that many of you will not be comfortable with my script, and that's okay. The important thing here is that you are comfortable and that you can express your self in a <u>natural way</u> to the person on the other end of the phone. Now think what is meant by the words "**Natural Way.**" We've all had the experience of unnatural people on the phone line haven't we? You know the idiots, **<u>theonesthatnevert akeabreathwhentheirtalkingorletyougetawordined gewise!</u>**

This has been one of the most destructive forces against the Insurance Agent. Telemarketers whose industry is now paying for their past sins. The problem is that we're paying for their sins too. This is why you must sound **human** when you are making those calls. Be a breath of fresh air to these people and you will not only set more quality appointments, but you'll make more friends. So don't be "a telemarketer," be a nice **human** for goodness sake, and just have a normal conversation with these people. They deserve it and you'll be happier and healthier because of it.

WORD OF CAUTION!! DON'T YOU DARE SAY

TO THESE PEOPLE WHEN THEY ANSWER THE PHONE:
"Hello, how are you doing today…!!!"
OR SOMETHING ELSE THAT SOUNDS LIKE A BOOBISH TELEMARKETER!!

Don't you hate it when people do that to you? You know immediately that they are a telemarketer and that they don't <u>really</u> care how you are doing. Don't do it to your potential clients!

What follows is the phone script that I have used for years. It's simple, effective, and does not take a ram it down your throat approach. It does assume that the people you are calling have responded to some type of solicitation, usually a mail in information request card. If you need a suggestion for a good lead company for long term care agents, I'll have contact information at the end of the book.

As you read through my phone script, you need to realize that it is written as a "perfect scenario." In real life this doesn't happen very often. What I am trying to accomplish here is to get you comfortable with the script. Client "objections" will be covered later. A gem of truth: ◊ It is important to <u>not</u> take a defensive approach when making calls, but to remain calm and relaxed. ◊ You have to believe in your heart that these people have requested information because they are truly interested in long term care insurance.

<u>MY SCRIPT,… A GOOD ONE!</u>
(*RING…RING…RING*) YES MAY I SPEAK WITH TOM JONES PLEASE? … HI MR.

JONES, MY NAME IS (*YOUR NAME*) **AND I'M WITH THE LONG TERM CARE DIVISION OF** (*YOUR COMPANY*) *SLIGHT-PAUSE*.

THE REASON FOR MY CALL, I RECEIVED THE CARD YOU MAILED IN A COUPLE OF WEEKS AGO REQUESTING INFORMATION ABOUT THE LONG TERM CARE PLAN THAT PAYS FOR HOME HEALTH CARE (*pause*)…**DO YOU RECALL THE CARD?**

SHUT-UP AND LET THEM ANSWER. DO NOT SPEAK UNTIL THEY ANSWER AND NO MATTER WHAT THEY SAY CONTINUE ON WITH THE NEXT PART

MR. JONES, THE REASON FOR MY CALL, I'M THE REPRESENTATIVE FOR (*YOUR COMPANY*) **IN** (*THEIR TOWN*) **AND I WAS HOPING TO FIND A TIME THIS WEEK TO _SWING BY_ WITH THAT INFORMATION AND SOME PRICING… WHICH WOULD BE BETTER FOR YOU, TUESDAY OR WEDNESDAY?…** (*PAUSE*) … **TUESDAY? …GREAT! WHAT'S BETTER, MORNING OR AFTERNOON?** (*LET THEM ANSWER*) **MORNING?...GREAT! HOW'S 10:00 AM? GREAT! OK …MR. JONES IF YOU COULD GRAB A PEN AND YOUR**

CALENDAR I'D LIKE TO LEAVE MY NAME WITH YOU SO YOU KNOW WHO TO EXPECT....GOT IT? GREAT. MY NAME IS *(YOUR NAME AND SPELL IT OUT. MY NAME IS UNUSUAL [VAHLE] SO I ALWAYS SAY SOMETHING LIKE, "SOUNDS LIKE VOLLEY IN VOLLEY BALL," I USUALLY GET A LAUGH.)*

MR. JONES, JUST A FEW QUICK QUESTIONS BEFORE I LET YOU GO... JUST WANTED TO FIRST VERIFY YOUR AGE AND BIRTHDATE... *(TAKE NOTES)* DO YOU TAKE ANY PRESCRIPTION MEDICATIONS? *(TAKE NOTES)* AND MAY I ASK WHAT YOU'RE BEING TREATED FOR? *(TAKE NOTES)* HAVE YOU BEEN IN THE HOSPITAL WITHIN THE PAST 5 YEARS FOR ANYTHING AT ALL? *(TAKE NOTES)*

OK, I THINK I HAVE ALL THE INFORMATION I NEED FOR NOW...I'VE GOT YOU DOWN FOR TUESDAY AT 10:00 AM AND I SHOULD BE PROMPT BUT IF YOU COULD GIVE ME A LITTLE LEEWAY IN CASE OF TRAFFIC I WOULD APPRECIATE IT. *(I ALSO LIKE TO ASK IF IT'S OKAY TO COME EARLY WHICH IS NICE ESPECIALLY IF YOU GET STOOD UP FROM A PREVIOUS APPOINTMENT)* AND I HAVE YOUR ADDRESS AS . . . .?

GREAT MR. JONES, THAT SHOULD DO IT...ONE LAST QUESTION BEFORE I LET YOU GO...HAVE YOU EVER KNOWN OF A FRIEND OR FAMILY MEMBER THAT HAS SPENT TIME IN A NURSING HOME OR NEEDED LONG TERM CARE? *(TAKE GOOD NOTES)* **OK, THAT SHOULD DO IT...SEE YOU TUESDAY...BYE!**

There it is...extremely simple and effective. I have trained numerous people with this script, including my wife, who by the way was the best "quality appointment setter" <u>ever</u>. In fact, my advice to you is to learn this script yourself, really get it down, and then train someone else to make your calls for you. A husband or wife is great and it's really strong when he or she say's, **"MY HUSBAND (OR WIFE) IS THE REPRESENTATIVE FOR XYZ COMPANY IN YOUR AREA."** For some reason that always seemed to connect with my clients. I would show up at their house and they would be warmed up and ready to talk because of the great job that my wife did for me.

But **<u>you</u>** have to learn this first! Don't think you can train somebody to set appointments if you yourself haven't been proven. There are many thoughts and ways as to how to get your appointments. Some LTC Agents never allow anyone to make calls for them. They feel that it is important to connect with the client personally before they meet with them. In time you will discover what works for you. Now we are laying a foundation of BASICS, someday you will build on that anyway you wish.

The purpose of asking the health questions is two fold. First, to determine if all options will be available to your client, and second, to determine if your client will even qualify. If dealing with a couple and one won't qualify, go to the appointment anyway. Don't tell them before hand that one won't qualify for a policy unless they ask.

Your script will be perfected through your own experience and the experience of others. For example, the deliberate choice of one word in the script is something that I gleaned through the experience of another agent. I use the word "swing" by instead of "drop" by and there is a good reason for that. There is an agent, whom I believe is absolutely one of the best ever in the history of LTC selling, who told me way back in 1990 how "swing by" was a much softer phrase to use and would yield a greater number of appointments. Your goal is to put potential clients at ease and "swing by" sounds better.

CHAPTER 3

ROLE PLAYING

Ah, role playing, oh joy. This is one of those things I always hated to participate in because I stunk at it. I hated it because it wasn't real. Having said that, we have to start somewhere and that somewhere is right here. My way of role playing though, is a little bit different than what is normally done. I believe in making it as real as possible.

The traditional way that it's done is in a group setting where everyone is watching you and the pressure is on. The guy or gal who is the smoothest talker puts everyone to shame as they dazzle the audience with their ability to remember the script. Guess what, that's not the way it is at all. Remember what I said earlier. It's all about hanging in there and persisting. Role playing "in class" is nothing more than horse hockey, if you catch my drift!

When you get out of class and you are alone in your home or office making calls, talking and having conversations with these wonderful seniors, that's what counts, not here, not now. My own experience went like this. The year was 1989 and it was myself and one other guy in class who was some insurance pro that had been around the block so to speak. The week of training consisted of pretty much nothing but role playing and I was just miserable at it. I found out later that by the end of the week he and my boss bet I wouldn't last. Wrong!

That was the first LTC Company that I worked for and I was there a little over eight years. When I left I had a great book of placed business. So relax and let's try to learn this script and get it into your bones as much as we can. The sooner we do that, the sooner we can throw this *script* away because the script will be inside you.

My belief is that if you are reading off of a piece of paper you're going to sound like you're reading off of a piece of paper, and that's not a good thing, it's not normal. When you talk to someone on the phone in your normal day to day life, how many times do you need a script? This flies in the face of many company philosophies, but it must be said.

Companies need to loosen up and realize that if they put their energy into helping agents be "real" on the phone they would stand to gain much in the way of business. Look at what is happening with the telemarketing industry and realize that the public is sick and tired of annoying script reading robots. Be "real" on the phone, and be successful.

GRAB A PARTNER

Everyone needs to grab somebody who can be Mr. Jones for you. Get off into some quiet spot and go through the phone script **without Mr. Jones giving any objections**. We want to start out nice and easy. We will cover objections later. You need to become comfortable with the process of going through the script, and being tripped up with objections at this point is nonsense. When you do this exercise, you need to concentrate on your "speech pace." I hate to belabor the point, but the goal is to get you to the place where you are real on the phone, not fake. Here we go.

Read through the script with effort being put into the <u>pace of the reading</u>, not so much what the script says. Remember, it's not *what* you say it's *how* you say it! Mr. Jones needs to be completely agreeable in all answers with no objections at this time. Also feel free to switch roles with each other every now and then.

Once you feel comfortable with the script, break the script down into an outline form or cheat sheet that you can glance at. By doing this, you will have to ad lib the script which will help you commit it to memory. You want to make it a part of you, rather than reading from a piece of paper. You are looking for a conversation that flows, not for a perfect set of words to read to someone. Here is an example of key phrases to glance at in order to stay on track and keep you moving forward through the conversation:

1. May I speak with . . .
2. Hi_____, my name is . . .
3. The reason for my call, I received . . .
4. Do you recall the card?
5. The reason for my call, I'm the representative . .
6. Hoping to find a time to swing by . . .

7. Which day would be better for you . . .*(time)*
8. _____, could you grab a pen and calendar
9. *Verify age, health conditions*
10. *Confirm appt. date, time, and their address*
11. _____, one last question . .*(experience w/ LTC)*

Now let's take the role playing to a level that's a bit more real if possible. You and your partner need to find a couple of phones and you the agent need to call Mr. Jones. Using your outline, set an appointment over the phone. This works great if you can be separated from each other in different rooms. It really gives a much more "real" feel and sensation to the exercise. Again, the object is to get comfortable with the process. Use the outline and just have a conversation with Mr. Jones.

CHAPTER 4

HANDLING PHONE OBJECTIONS

Once you are comfortable with the script then you are ready to incorporate the dreaded objections. In a minute we will look at some of the most common objections and <u>simple</u> responses to them. First though, here is a gem of truth: ◊ An objection does not require a *detailed* response, but a *simple answer* and a continuation of the appointment setting process. ◊ In other words, answer the objection and move on.

Some sales people are constantly talking themselves out of sales opportunities. They feel they must always be talking, talking, talking! Here is another gem of truth: ◊ Let your response be determined by listening closely, then speaking. ◊ The great salesmen know how to concentrate on what's being said, process it, and *then* answer. But they also do something else. They constantly maintain control and move forward, or in other words, **they are always closing.**

A great closer in action is something to behold. It's like a basketball player bringing the ball up the court weaving through defenders. At the appropriate time he is able to take it strong to the hoop, then dunking.

It looks and feels good. So if you catch my drift, the issue here is not the words you answer the objections with, but <u>your ability</u> to continue forward motion (i.e.) **setting the appointment**. This is really the million dollar question. Will you be able to move through objections while assuming you've got the appointment, or bluntly speaking can you deflect the objection and set the appointment anyway? I know for some that haven't been in sales, this may sound crazy or even like trickery. I assure you it isn't.

You are facing a situation in which most people, given the choice, do not want you in the home and are looking for any opportunity <u>to not set up an appointment</u> with you. It's up to you to be more determined than they are.

Determination and perseverance, this is what's needed. So often we mistakenly think that perseverance is walking forward and not stopping, wrong! God gave you two legs to walk and walking is natural and requires nothing extra. No, I would say a better definition of perseverance would be walking and not being detoured by someone standing in your way. *That* requires something extra. Everyone with two legs can walk, but not everyone can persevere. What about you?

Remember, no matter where an objection comes during the phone call it changes nothing, you answer and go on. Here are some of the most common objections and simple answers for them. See if you can come up with some of your own. Just remember to keep your responses short. Again, the goal is to keep moving forward until the appointment is scheduled. Here's a gem of truth: ◊ The more real and natural you are on the phone, the less you will have to deal with objections. ◊

I THOUGHT THEY WERE GOING TO MAIL IT-1

YES THAT'S WHY I WAS CALLING. MR. JONES, I AM THE REPRESENTATIVE FOR . . . .AND I WAS HOPING TO FIND A GOOD TIME TO SWING BY WITH THAT INFORMATION . . .

I THOUGHT THEY WERE GOING TO MAIL IT-2

THE INFORMATION THAT I MAIL DOES NOT CONTAIN ANY PRICING, WERE YOU WANTING TO KNOW THE COST?

I THOUGHT THEY WERE GOING TO MAIL IT-3

WHAT WERE YOU HOPING TO RECEIVE?

I'M NOT INTERESTED-1

I NOTICED ON THE CARD YOU MAILED IN, THAT IT TALKED ABOUT THE COST OF LONG TERM CARE IN THE U.S.. WAS THAT WHAT CAUSED YOU TO BECOME INTERESTED IN LTC INSURANCE?

I'M NOT INTERESTED-2

I UNDERSTAND, MOST PEOPLE ARE NOT INTERESTED IN SPENDING THEIR ASSETS IN A NURSING HOME. IS THAT WHAT INSPIRED YOU TO SEND IN FOR INFORMATION?

I'M TOO BUSY-1

I UNDERSTAND, THAT'S WHY WHEN I SAW THE PHONE NUMBER THAT YOU GAVE US ON THE CARD I WANTED TO CALL YOU BEFORE I STOPPED BY...WHAT'S USALLY THE BEST TIME OF THE DAY FOR YOU...MORNING OR AFTERNOON?

I'M **TOO BUSY-2**

I UNDERSTAND. THAT'S WHY I WANTED TO GET HOLD OF YOU. I HAVE BEEN VERY BUSY BUT HAVE ANOTHER APPOINTMENT IN YOUR AREA THIS WEEK AND WAS HOPING TO SWING BY WHILE I HAD THE CHANCE. WHAT'S BETTER, MONDAY OR TUESDAY?

I'M **TOO BUSY-3**

OK, I UNDERSTAND. NORMALLY WHAT IS THE BEST TIME OF DAY FOR YOU?

KIDS WILL TAKE CARE OF ME-1

GREAT! THAT'S WHY I WAS CALLING. THE PLANS THAT ARE NOW AVAILBLE ARE DESIGNED FOR YOUR CHILDREN TO HELP THEM TAKE CARE OF YOU. WHICH DAY IS BEST SUITED FOR ME TO SWING BY, MONDAY OR TUESDAY?

KIDS WILL TAKE CARE OF ME-2

GREAT! IT'S ALWAYS NICE WHEN THE KIDS AND GRANDKIDS ARE INVOLVED IN THE CARE OF MOM AND DAD. DID YOU TAKE CARE OF YOUR PARENTS?

THE GOVERNMENT WILL TAKE CARE OF ME-1

YES! THAT'S WHY I'M CALLING. SO YOU'VE HEARD ABOUT THE FEDERALY TAX QUALIFIED PLANS NOW AVAILABLE?

THE GOVERNMENT WILL TAKE CARE OF ME-2

WELL YES! SO YOU'VE HEARD ABOUT THE NEW GOVERNMENT TAX QUALIFIED PLANS?

Is this simplistic? Yes it is, and some of the responses even seem a little goofy, but they work. Let me be very clear, they work because you are determined to set an appointment, not because the answer is cutesy or tricky. Most people have a programmed response within them when a salesman wants to come by...**a programmed response**. Hold a lit match to your hand and you'll get the same response every single time. Ahhhhhhhh! It's no different when you call. You have to help move them past that initial programmed response. Remember the gem: ◊ No matter what the objection, you just keep plowing ahead. ◊

If you have someone that keeps bringing up one objection after another, then you need to use the Socratic Method. This is nothing more than answering a question with a question. It is extremely effective. The more you can get these people talking, the more they begin to remember why they decided to mail that card back or respond to that advertisement.

You will find it extremely frustrating to call a lead of whatever source only to hear them say they are not interested and yet you know they just sent the information card back a week ago. Whatever you do, don't argue! In those situations, use the Socratic Method and get them talking and remembering, it works!

I will also share one of my codes that I live by. ◊ Never burn a bridge unless you absolutely have to. ◊ I can't tell you how many times through the years that I have gotten somebody on a bad day and called them two weeks later and set the appointment either with them or their spouse. You can ask any experienced agent and they will all have a similar story they could share along those lines. We all have bad days, so make sure you are extremely gracious and you won't go wrong.

HERE IS THE GOOD NEWS!!

The good news is that no matter how many objections you get, you will still set all the appointments you want. That's right all you want…and how do I know that? It is very simple and it involves the truth about numbers. Numbers do not lie. Here we go, pick up the phone and dial it enough to get fifty people to **answer the phone**. You will then set eight to ten appointments every single week, and that is being conservative. If you want more just dial more. No matter how weak you may be on the phone it doesn't make a hill of beans difference because it works for everyone. The numbers are with you, you should be very encouraged.

CHAPTER 5

BEFORE THE HOME INTERVIEW

BASIC AGENT HYGIENE AND DRESS

Go ahead and laugh. You would think we wouldn't have to talk about this. Well my friends, all I can say is that it is sometimes necessary. Look, it's hard enough out there without ruining that sale because your breath is bad, so let's discuss it, shall we? Gem of truth ◊ There are many things that arc out of your control… don't sweat those. The things that are in your control. . . change those for the better.◊

Everyone has a different idea of what proper dress is. My idea has always been to dress with a coat and tie and look sharp. Others feel you should dress as the client dresses, which means business casual for the most part. There are good arguments on either side. I think the main thing is to not take short cuts and be lazy. In other words, pay attention to how you look and know this, your clients do.

One big plus to working in an agency is the accountability factor. Having someone to answer to helps keep you on your toes in all facets of the business, including dress and hygiene, so you're less likely to let yourself go in that area. But I'm sure as you read this probably half of you think you can be a good ole boy and your country charm will be more than enough to make that sale, and there are those out there that can back it up. But for most of us, this is something worth paying attention to.

Here are some things to keep in mind before you go out and meet the people.

1. LOOK CLEAN AND PRETTY WITH SHOES SHINED AND SHIRT TUCKED IN. (Also pay a couple of bucks to have the cleaners do your shirt. You look tacky when it's wrinkled.)

2. NAILS TRIMMED (It's amazing how people will judge you by your nails.)

3. USE A BREATH MINT, ESPECIALLY IF YOU SMOKE (If you smoke, it's not a bad idea to put on a little cologne before walking in.)

4. MAKE SURE YOUR CAR IS CLEAN INSIDE AND OUT. (Many times through the years clients have walked me out to the car after the sale. Sometimes it's just to check you out further.)

These things may seem really nit picky, but the senior population has a different way of looking at things. They're not nearly as loose and free about things. They believe that when things are not done in a certain way you show a lack of respect. This is how they were raised and we need to take note of that. Personally, I think we need more of that today.

LOOKS LIKE WE'RE READY TO DO AN INTERVIEW!

CHAPTER 6

AT THE DOOR

You understand the product, you've made the call, and you've set the appointment. So here you are…at the door. Now the fun begins. Now you find out how well you prequalified and if they are ready to see you. Let me walk you through the process with some common sense tips along the way.

1. TAKE EVERYTHING YOU NEED TO MAKE A SALE <u>WITH YOU</u> INTO THE HOME. DON'T OVERKILL BUT LOOK PROFESSIONAL AND BE PREPARED.

2. SMILE AS YOU APPROACH THE HOUSE. YOU MIGHT NOT SEE THEM BUT THEY COULD BE CHECKING YOU OUT. ALSO, SOME PEOPLE LIKE TO PRETEND THEY ARE NOT HOME, SO IT'S IMPORTANT TO SMILE AS IF YOU SEE THEM. SOME AGENTS AUTOMATICALLY WAVE AT THE HOUSE.

3. MAKE THE FIRST IMPRESSION A GOOD ONE. SMILE AS YOU INTRODUCE YOURSELF.

4. WITH CONFIDENCE WIPE YOUR FEET ON THE DOORMAT BECAUSE YOU KNOW THEY'RE EXPECTING YOU AND YOU'RE COMING IN THE HOUSE. MAKE IT A POINT TO SHAKE HANDS AND LOOK THEM IN THE EYE.

5. NO MATTER WHO LETS YOU IN THE HOUSE, ALWAYS STAND WHEN THE OTHER SPOUSE COMES INTO THE ROOM HOLDING OUT YOUR HAND AS YOU INTRODUCE YOURSELF. THIS USED TO BE COMMON COURTESY. IT ALWAYS SURPRISES AND IMPRESSES.

6. IF THEY ASK WHERE YOU WOULD LIKE TO SIT, ALWAYS CHOOSE THE TABLE. IF THEY MOTION YOU INTO THE LIVING ROOM, THAT'S FINE, BECAUSE YOU WILL END UP AT THE TABLE SOON ENOUGH. IF YOU DETECT NERVOUSNESS ALWAYS SAY, "WHEREVER YOU'RE MOST COMFORTABLE." IT PUTS THEM AT EASE.

Ok you've make a great first impression, you are seated and ready to go. Relax and let's have fun!

CHAPTER 7

HOW TO DO THE HOME INTERVIEW

FROM START→TO FINISH...THE OUTLINE:
Remember that even though you want to establish a good relationship with the client for obvious reasons, you are there to **sell!** I have walked out of many homes before without a sale and yet the client says, "Oh you did such a lovely job." Yeah right I'm thinking, if I did such a lovely job why didn't you take out a policy? Again, please don't misunderstand me. ◊ I want a relationship, but I also want to have a sale. I'm going to make lots of friends, but I want to make a living. ◊

This brings me to an observation that I have made as I have listened to many an agent through the years. The claim has been made by some that, "Oh I just want to help people and the money is not important." as if the money is secondary to which I say BS. If you expect me or any other clear thinking person to believe that, you've got another thing coming, and further more I don't want you working for me! Use the same statement with any other occupation in America and you'll see my point. Can you imagine a gas station attendant telling his boss, "Oh I don't want to sell gas I just love giving people directions." He wouldn't dare. Or a teacher saying, "Oh I don't want to teach, I just love making kids happy." You see it makes no sense at all. Yes you have a mission, and yes you do the best job for the customer. That's a <u>given</u> for crying out loud. Make no mistake though, you are a LTC *Salesman.*

Ok, let's begin by looking at an outline of the sales process. You will want to put this to memory but only as a foundation to guide you. After a while you will have your own words and style that are truly yours and yours alone; words borne from your own experiences. Please take these words to heart: ◊ You do not want to memorize what to say. You want to work on how you express yourself to Mr. and Mrs. Jones. ◊ By the time we are done you're going to be sick of me saying this, but this is *very* important. You are trying to make a connection with these people and these people are smart. They have been around the block and have heard it all before. So you have to speak with **passion and smarts** at the same time. As long as they can see that you will have success. Remember the good news about the phone calling? The same goes for numbers of appointments. Even the worst salesman will have success as long as he is consistently working eight to ten appointments per week.

One last thing before we get to the outline. Use your weakness as a new agent as a tremendous strength. The Apostle Paul said that when he was weak then he was strong because he did not rely on the strength of men but of God. When you are just starting, don't be afraid to tell these people you are brand new in the LTC business. They will tend to be softer on rookies. Also, if you act like a know it all they'll see right through it and then you're dead meat. As long as you've got a story to tell with passion, you will do fine. More on that later. Here we go with the outline.

1. Warm up period.
2. Confirmation of information.
3. Why you? Why today?
4. LTC experience with family and friends- how would you pay?
5. My LTC story, why I'm in the business.
6. My goal today, setting the agenda.
7. Confirm the assets.
8. Design the program.
9. Fill out the application, paperwork, and collect the check.
10. Go through the brochure.
11. Get referrals.
12. Leave information and make delivery arrangements.

Many of you are thinking my goodness, there is no way I can remember this! Yes you can because I did it, and as a former butcher that's saying a lot. Before we break this outline down point by point, you need to know that you don't go through all of this unless Mr. and Mrs. Jones are buying. As a rule <u>I do not go past point number six</u> unless they are buying. On occasion I have, but rarely. The best advice for rookies is to go out, have fun and do as many appointments as you can to increase your comfort level with the process. In time you will find the ability to detect the right signals that indicate "THEY WANT A POLICY."

CHAPTER 8

THE SALES PITCH BREAKDOWN POINT BY POINT

1. Warm-up period. The warm-up starts the moment you get out of your car and is the most important part of the sales process. It's where you are sizing up the client and the client is deciding whether or not they like and trust you, so you had better be on your toes. You must do your best to be genuinely interested in them. Don't be too aggressive at this point, but ask a lot of questions because you want *them* to talk. Surprise them by not living up to the stereotypes of the "insurance agent." Oh how insurance people love to talk and boast as anyone who has been to an insurance convention will be able to tell you. This meeting is about them. You gain trust when you ask about them, their family, and the ever popular grandkids. Here are some pointers to keep you on the right track.

- Give a good hand shake while looking them in the eye.
- Look sharp and smell good.

- Be warm, concentrating on them and their life, not yours.
- Start the conversation off with small talk. "How long have you lived here, how many children and grandchildren, what did you do for a living?" Take a look at the walls and what's hanging on them to get an idea of their interests. If you get them talking, conversation won't be a problem.
- If they're not too talkative, it may be that they want to get started, so be sensitive to that. You may want to share a little bit about yourself and family. Just control the urge to babble.
- ◊ Let your gut be your guide, it does not lie. ◊ When you feel everyone is comfortable and relaxed you are then ready for the next step.

2. Confirmation of Information. It is very important that you do thorough work here. This is where you will begin to decide what company or product you are going to sell to them. Contrary to some opinion; ◊ You the Agent decide what the client is going to buy. The good agent, however, makes them think they are the ones making all the decisions. ◊ Much of the time the decision as to which company to go with is already determined by the health information you've obtained, but reconfirm everything. ◊ The number one problem we face today is the health situation of the client and being able to place the clients business, not the cost of the insurance as some so called experts say. ◊ This is how I confirm their information.

- "Mr. and Mrs. Jones, before we get started, I want to make sure I've got your age and birth date marked correctly."
- "When we spoke on the phone, you gave me some information concerning your health. Let me verify that information." *Be sure to ask about the last five years and get all the details; medications, hospitalizations, diabetes, stroke, TIA's, etcetera.* "I know these are personal questions, and I appreciate you sharing that information with me, but let me share with you how a long term care policy is approved. First, we get the name, address, and phone number of your family doctor. Next we fill out a brief questionnaire concerning your health history in the past five years. We turn that information into the XYZ Insurance Company along with the "almighty premium check." It usually takes four to six weeks for them to issue the policy. If God forbid they don't approve you, the premium check is refunded in full."

This issue concerning the premium check may have to be repeated several times throughout the appointment. You want to make sure they hear that a premium is collected with the application so that there are no surprises at the closing. Nothing is more frustrating than getting the application filled out, asking for the check and seeing your prospective client in shock because they didn't know that they had to pay anything down. If they're going to object to writing a check you want to hear about it early on so you can deal with it now rather than later. You'll find though, that with the more experience you gain, collecting the check will become less of a problem.

- Confirm anything else that you spoke about on the phone such as the mention of a friend or family member that needed long term care.

Here is another helpful sales nugget: ◊ Do a lot of writing with each health condition they mention, nodding as you go. Do a lot of hmmm sounds keeping a serious expression on your face. ◊ It is important to be very animated when taking the health information. We have to get across to our clients that the biggest obstacle to getting LTC insurance is the health issue, not the cost. When we walk in the door, *their* concern is "how much is this going to cost." We have to take away their fears of cost and show them their vulnerability concerning health. Have you ever been to a play? Ever notice how made up all the actors are? They are very animated. They do this to make sure they are seen and noticed. In the very same way, we must be seen and heard. We have a limited time to make our case regarding the importance of the health issue, and we have to make it good.

3. Why you? Why today? Now we're beginning to get into the meat. We've collected valuable information, were feeling comfortable, and we should be getting to know these people by now. At this point you may already have an idea if these folks are buyers or not, but don't count your money yet. Take it slow and easy and don't be fooled by a lot of emotion.

PAUSE, LOOK THEM IN THE EYE...AND SAY...

- "Mr. and Mrs. Jones when you mailed this card back," (*or when you responded to whatever*) "what were you thinking about?"

THEN SHUT-UP, LISTEN, AND TAKE NOTES!
When they are done you can ask:

- "Why have you waited so long to look into LTC insurance?"

If you think you're being direct, you're right… you are. This is an **awful subject**. This is not a shiny red sports car that you're selling, and you have to be strong without being over bearing; in their face without offending. For the client that thinks the kids are going to be there for them, you are looking for a polite way to say, "How would you feel about your son-in-law having to hold the shit from your diaper in his hands?" Of course, I have never said that, nor should anyone ever be so rude, but that's the dilemma we face. ◊ We have a responsibility to speak the truth in love. That sometimes calls for a *teensy* bit of pain, but never to be rude or offensive. ◊

I know of agents that behave like a bull in a china shop. They think that *their* knowledge of the *risk* of needing LTC insurance somehow gives them the right to offend. If you have to offend to sell, you're in the wrong business. The point of "Why you? Why now?" is to begin to hear their story, ask questions, and then move into the next point.

4. LTC experience with family and friends-how would you pay? We are trying to build on what we've started. We are beginning to hear what's in their heart, that is… we hope we are. What you are doing is building a case for LTC insurance *with their help.* Contrary to what many in the business think, you cannot build on something that isn't there. ◊ It has been said that, "We as agents must create need." to which I say no, "We expose the need that is already there." ◊ You want these people to sell themselves, bringing out thoughts and emotions relating to LTC in their own life and family. This is the way to do it. To say that we can create in them the need to buy implies some kind of hocus pocus or false pretense. People will do what is in them to do and nothing further.

So to review: (1) We've warmed them up and gotten to know them better and we have (2) confirmed vital statistics. We have also begun to (3) find out some deep reasons as to why we might be there, or at the least begun to have a sense of why we're there. Now we (4) probe even deeper into family and friends LTC experience history. This is where we begin to lock down or *affirm in them inwardly* that we're doing something here and now, and most important to you the Agent; <u>TODAY!</u>

Now you've already heard about their family situation and their LTC story from the last part. We just want to lock down their story so that we know it and so that they can't get it out of their mind. They must take ownership and admit this could happen to them just as it did with one of their loved ones. This is the reason for all the questions, they are telling you why you're there. If you can't nail down why you're there then you can forget about selling a policy. Here is an obvious but sobering nugget of truth: ◊ The best sales tool we have is their bad experience. You are looking for a bad experience. ◊ It's sad but very true. That is why when you go into the home this information of who, what, when, where, why, and how is vital to the sale and without it a sale will probably not happen.

Pencil pushers that have never been out in the field and made a sales call believe that information sells LTC insurance. Wrong, wrong, wrong! Purchasing LTC insurance is like dying or worse for some people. It's a resignation of their mortality that they don't want to face. Talking about losing their independence and declining health is a god awful subject not easily approached unless someone has had personal experience. Only by moving their experience into the realm of their immediate family (them, their kids, and grandkids) will they be pushed into the sales arena. So… you want to be taking good notes on their bad experiences. If necessary, these can be thrown back in their face with the hope that they will own up to the truth that it could happen to them. Here are some basic questions to cover making sure you get details from both sides of the family.

- "Who needed long term care?"
- "How long did they need it?"
- "How much did it cost?"
- "Did the family take part in their care?"
- "How did this affect the family as a whole?"
- "What illness were they suffering from?"
- "Does it run in the family?"

This list could go on and on. There is no end to the questions you can ask and the strong case that you can build for LTC insurance. Ok, you've gotten all this information of tremendous value, you're building a wonderful case, and now the time has come to insert some <u>dagger questions</u> that will help show you the way to the sale or to the door.

- "Do you want the same situation for your children and grandchildren as you had?"
- "If you needed long term care today...who would care for you?"
- "If you needed long term care today how would you pay for it?"

If while listening you get the impression that the children are very involved and could be a problem, then you need to ask this next question. Otherwise move on to the next point.

- "What do you think your children would say if they knew you were looking into LTC insurance?"

It is extremely important that you listen carefully. It is my strong opinion that children can be the biggest obstacle to Mr. and Mrs. Jones taking out LTC insurance. Many children have sold their parents on the idea that they will take care of them if they ever need long term care. If the clients are convinced that their children are going to be there to care for them, then it's time to turn up the heat just a little bit. Ask these questions, "Mr. and Mrs. Jones, if you needed long term care today, right now, which one of your children is prepared to drop everything and care for you round the clock? How would you feel about that? Do they have a family? Do they work? Do they live here in the area?" At this point, if you feel that they are still convinced their children can care for them round the clock, then it's time for a gutsy move.

Very politely thank them for allowing you to come into their home and meet them, but it looks like XYZ Insurance Company has nothing to offer them. Pull out a business card and say, "If you ever feel differently, and your children are not your solution for long term care, then I would love to come back and share with you how XYZ Insurance Company has solved the problem of long term care for so many people, and at the same time protected their assets. Thank you again; it has been a pleasure meeting you." Remember, be extremely gracious, because you never know, you may get a chance to get back into the home. It's better to find out now if the children are a stopper than at the end of the appointment.

5. My LTC story, why I'm in the business. Even though you've been closing throughout the appointment, now things are really heating up and the tone is more focused to an end. The past four stages have been information stages designed to mold Mr. and Mrs. Jones for the actual close of the sale. If you're still sitting there with the client and have gotten past point four and collected all that information, that's very good news. You would much rather be told to leave in the information stage than at the end when you've spent a good amount of energy and time.

That's why all the questions, you are provoking them to respond one way or the other. If you get in a home and the prospects are not willing to answer your questions and all they want is the price, I have one word of advice, LEAVE! Don't be sucked into giving up the gold so easily. A great story told to me years ago by an agent that I worked with in the Indianapolis area, concerned an appointment he had scheduled earlier in the week. When he arrived at the prospects home, the gentleman was outside on a ladder painting or working, I can't remember which. Anyway, when the agent went up to the man and introduced himself, the man made it clear that he had no intention of going inside and could the agent just give him a price. The agent friend of mine spoke with a firm courtesy and told the gentleman that he was a professional and not a brush salesman. The man looked him over, got down off the ladder and motioned toward the house. When they sat down at the table the gentleman looked the agent in the eye and said, "I was a brush salesman." The end result was a sale for that agent, and a great example for the rest of us not to give in but to be willing to stand firm and be a professional.

So many agents are intimidated and easily manipulated by the older and wiser prospects with the end result being failure. You've got to be able to look people in the eye and not sweat a drop. Here at point five you have an opportunity to show the passion you have about LTC insurance and why you are in the business. To do this effectively you need a story, and hopefully one that is your own. You've got to be able to put into words what happened to someone who needed long term care but did not have any insurance to pay for it. What happened to the family, how it affected everything, what a tremendous burden it was. You've got to wake these people out of their sleep. An emotional personal story from you is just what is needed, one straight from the heart. You can begin like this.

- "Mr. and Mrs. Jones, I appreciate you sharing with me your experiences and all the health information. I want to share with you how I got into the long term care business and why I believe in long term care insurance."

At this point tell them about yourself. How you got into the business, how long you've been in the business, just don't over kill. You really have to fight the temptation to talk about yourself; you need to focus on them. Use your inexperience as a weapon and please be honest about it. Don't portray yourself as a "know it all" if you don't…know it all. Share with passion your personal LTC story or a couple of short long term care lack of insurance stories you have heard.

You'll find in most cases that these people have the same stories already in their mind. So be confident when bringing up this uncomfortable subject. Your clients have lived a lot longer and have many real life long term care situations already in mind. Remember, if you knocked on every door in your town and asked the question, "Have you ever known of someone in your family or a friend that has needed long term care?" over 90% of the people will say yes. Those that don't either aren't telling, or they don't remember. I can't tell you how many times through the years that someone would tell me that they know of no one that needed long term care, only to remember half way through the appointment someone that they had forgotten about. It happened time after time. Once you've told them your story you're now ready to move on…deeper.

6. My goal today, setting the agenda. One of the marks of a super salesman is his or her ability to take control of the meeting and point it in the direction of their choosing. ◊ The Mr. and Mrs. Joneses of the world respect a take charge person if they feel they are being directed <u>under consent</u>. ◊ As you move through each one of these points and are able to continue, that's the consent and permission you need, and you should move ahead with confidence. As you allow this presentation to become a part of you, you will become comfortable with it and you will be able to move and close with confidence. Remember though, this ability to close is only accomplished by experience, not by book knowledge or role playing. This is why I keep encouraging every new agent to set as many appointments as possible, get in front of as many people as possible, and just have fun. Get to know people and learn by experience and you will be successful no matter how inept you may think you are. Some of the goofiest, strangest agents out there are also some of the most successful because they know about the law of numbers, which is simply the more people I'm in front of, the more chances I have to sell. It's that pure and simple. Here at point six you are ready to "set the agenda" and continue to pave the way for the physical closing.

- "Mr. and Mrs. Jones, my goal here today is to design a program that will not only protect your savings and assets but will also provide the peace of mind that you desire (*pause*). However, I have two concerns as I look and consider the information you've provided me. Number one, I want to make sure that this plan is designed so that it will not be a financial burden to you in any way. The good news is that there are many ways we can design your particular plan. Promise me though, that you will not consider anything that might be close to the edge financially, okay?" *Nod your head while looking at them and wait until you get a response. No matter what they say you continue on.*

- "The other concern and probably the biggest concern is the health information that you've shared with me. I don't believe at this point that they will turn you down, but I want to make sure we have as much information as possible, and more importantly what your doctor thinks of your health. When you last saw him what were his comments to you concerning your condition? (*pause and listen*) Do you think he feels good about your health? (*pause and listen*) You see, the biggest problem we face in the long term care industry is not the cost of these policies but qualifying people based on their health. Let me again explain how the process will work. Once we design the right program for you, we fill out a very simple questionnaire concerning your health. Next we get your doctors name, address, and phone number and we submit this information to XYZ Insurance Company along with the "almighty premium check" (*Pause and look directly at them nodding your head as you do.*) It usually takes four to six weeks before the policy is issued. During that time it is important that you STAY HEALTHY. Once it is issued, I will personally deliver it and you will have to sign a receipt of delivery which puts it into effect. Hopefully you'll never need to use it. Just like your auto, homeowners,

and major medical insurance, you hope
you never have to collect. Any questions
so far? (*pause and listen*)"

Once again this is where the rubber meets the road. You will learn a lot by pausing and listening, and again be either closer to the door or an application with a check. Remember, it's not what you say, it's how you say it. Timing is so important. Don't rush, look directly at them, notice their body language, <u>what are they saying to you</u>? You are now ready for the next step in this journey.

7. Confirm the assets. The fact that I confirm assets here and not at the beginning is based on my experiential gut feeling that they have assets to work with. If I doubt their ability to afford the insurance when I walk in the door, I qualify them financially when I health qualify. If I doubt their ability when I'm on the phone setting the appointment, I qualify them then and do not wait. Remember you don't want to spin your wheels, if there is any doubt early on...ASK.

I have met many agents through the years that have a real problem asking the client questions about money and many in fact don't. My opinion is, if you can't talk to them about money you might as well get out of the business now and stop wasting your time and everyone else's. ◊ The bottom line is that this long term care insurance business is all about money; the client's money and their family's inheritance. ◊ You need to act like a professional and get over any silly fear you have about talking to your clients about money. The interesting thing is that it's so easy to get the information you need just by being gracious. Once again, it's not what you ask it's how you ask it. After you've paused and listened at point six continue with:

- "Mr. and Mrs. Jones, before we can design an appropriate plan for both of you, I need to ask you a few personal questions. As you know, one of the main reasons people are buying LTC insurance is that they want to protect their money and assets. Unfortunately, sometimes people are buying LTC insurance when they don't need it. So if I may, I would like to ask you a couple of questions to determine if the two of you should even be considering this type of coverage, okay?" *Pause and let them answer. Get their permission to continue, and be sure to take good notes.*
- "To begin with, you own your home, right? And it's paid for? If you were going to estimate the value of your home what would a low ball amount be? Do you own any rental properties?" *Write down the estimated values.*
- "Now you're income is made up of what sources? Social Security? Pension? Interest income? Total monthly amount is?" *Again, write down the information.*
- "Lastly, if you took all the savings that you have and by savings I mean regular savings accounts, IRA's, annuities, stocks, bonds, etc. and added the amount up,

would it be above or below $100,000?"
Write down everything they give you.

Since 1989, rarely has anyone ever refused to give me the information I asked for. You just need to be courteous, direct, and professional when you ask. They will give it to you. Now you are ready to design the plan. If you are not sitting at a table, now is a good time to request to do so. Make sure you position yourself to be sitting across from Mr. and Mrs. Jones, not in between them.

8. Design the program. You are now ready to design the perfect plan for Mr. and Mrs. Jones and shine once again. Through the years I can't tell you how many times people have told me how much more impressed they were with me versus the other guy who came in first. I'm convinced that one of the reasons was that I was able to sell the right amount of coverage for their needs. Since I had knowledge of their assets, I didn't over or under sell. A huge problem that exists with many agents both new and not so new is that they don't meet the need of the customer. They sell cookie cutter plans, or one size fits all. Not only does the agent deserve a kick in the pants, but the company that sent that agent out deserves one too.

You've been given a tremendous opportunity to look at the financial situation of these people and you have an obligation to put together a correct plan and not screw it up. Now granted, what I believe is the perfect coverage, others may disagree with and that's fine. ◊ It's important for you to know why you as the agent sold a particular plan and to be able to explain yourself with some logic attached. ◊

I'll give you a great example of what some agents sell as appropriate coverage and the fallacy of it. As I go through this chapter, I will be using pricing reflective of the Midwest where I live. If you are on the East or West coast the price will obviously be higher. Let's say that the average cost of a long term care facility in Mr. and Mrs. Jones' area is $170 per day, not uncommon in the Midwest. Let's also assume that they are in their 50's. Mr. and Mrs. Jones are looking to the agent, whom they trust, to protect their assets both now and in the future. An agent comes in and sells them a flat $200 per day benefit with no inflation protection. Unfortunately, the agent doesn't have a clue.

Although there is enough coverage for the Jones' today, their policy will more likely be needed in the future. Then they are going to be up the creek with only half a paddle. Let's look ahead just 20 years, when they will be in their 70's. Assuming there is only a 5% simple increase per year in the cost of providing long term care, the cost of a LTC facility will increase in twenty years to $400 per day. This means that Mr. and Mrs. Jones will have to come up with $200 every day out of their own pocket, and the amount will continue to increase each year.

Now if your clients are determined to opt for a plan with no inflation protection there is not much you can say, but it might be in your best interest to get something in writing from them stating that fact. When they are in the nursing home and using their policy, I can almost guarantee the kids are going to want to know why their parents were sold such a low daily benefit on a policy that was supposed to protect assets and pay for their care.

So what is the correct daily benefit amount for your client? How long should their plan pay for long term care? What about an elimination period? In a minute we will go through everything step by step, but before that let's focus on the job at hand. Think about where you are. Consider what has happened within the past hour. You have met and gotten to know some wonderful people who have opened up in such a way that they may have shared things with you that their own family is not aware of. You need to be mindful of the trust that has been given you as you go forward into the designing of their plan and treat these people with the respect you would want for yourself and your family. So let's get started and do it right. Help them add the missing link to their financial situation!

Another gem that I feel is extremely helpful: ◊ When designing plans and comparing options, use a lap top computer complete with software provided by the companies that sell LTC insurance. ◊ Have it up and running on the table along with a large pad of paper and a good pen. I love using the computer because it makes you look professional and will increase their trust of you when they see the name and or logo of a well known company on the screen. To top that off, the computer ensures that you won't make any mistakes on pricing. Agents are known for making tons of pricing errors, and it's only because they are doing many things at the same time. Using a computer with your company's software helps eliminate mistakes.

The policy you sell your client may have provisions that cover assisted living facilities, home care, etc., but it is important that clients realize the financial impact of their worst fear; having to go to a nursing home. As I lead you through the scenarios of designing LTC policy plans, remember that I will be working with figures appropriate for the Midwest. You will need to make adjustments for the area in which you live. This is how you approach the daily benefit.

Daily Benefit

- "Mr. and Mrs. Jones, the first thing we need to do in order to figure out how much your plan is going to cost, is to decide how much you would like XYZ Insurance Company to pay you for each day you need care. The way we figure this is we look at the worst case scenario; if one of you had to go to a nursing home. We know that ABC Nursing Home runs $170 per day right now, or $5100 per month. My question to the both of you is; if one of you had to go into a nursing home next month, would you want XYZ Insurance Company to pay 100% of the cost or do you feel that you could pay part of the cost out of your own pocket?"

This is really worth spending some time on, and this is where they will see the difference between you and some other agent that may have already been in the home. If I'm in a home that I know was already visited by another agent, my antenna goes up. Much of the time the other agent quoted too high of a premium, at least in these folks mind, and they were scared off by it. So I go slow here and show them how they can bring down the cost of their policy by coinsuring.

I can't tell you how many times I've made someone's day by showing them the beauty of this way of thinking. It's usually, "Wow, the other guy didn't tell us we could do that!" or, "Look how much that will save us each year!" With the average cost of LTC policies approaching $2000 per year per individual, it's worth taking your time and saving them some serious dollars. ◊ Coinsuring, if done correctly, is a wonderful option for many people. ◊

- "Let me show you what I mean." *Grab your pad with their monthly income.* "Your income, which includes Social Security and a pension, adds up to $4000 per month."
- "Quick question Mr. Jones, if you God forbid had a stroke, and it was impossible for you to be taken care of in your home even with help brought in, and you had to go into ABC Nursing Home, how much would Mrs. Jones need every month to continue to live comfortably here in this home?"

Again, write everything down that they tell you. You are trying to determine if they can afford anything out of their pocket without changing their standard of living. Let me restate that: You are trying to determine if they can afford any of the cost of care out of their own pocket without changing their standard of living. It just makes sense to pay for part of your long term care if the money is there. Also, always include inflation protection in their plan. As mentioned earlier, without it you are building a plan that may not be equipped to do the job it was intended to do down the road. The only time I may not include it is when the client is advanced in age and it may make the cost of the plan prohibitive. In that case do the best you can with the dollars you have to work with. Something is better than nothing in the way of protection.

- "Mr. and Mrs. Jones, it looks like what you've shared with me indicates that Mrs. Jones would need $2500 per month to live comfortably here in your home if you weren't able to be here, and that you could easily afford $1000 per month out of your own pocket toward the cost of care without touching any interest. Let me explain why this might be the way to go. Both of you are spending income now, right? If you just changed your address and were living at the nursing home, you're still going to have income, right? If you're spending income includes traveling, going out to dinner, etc., why not use that income to help pay part of the cost of care if one of you were in a nursing home?"
- "Isn't the main reason we are talking today centered on the protection of your assets?

Not income, but assets, right? Now if you want XYZ Insurance Company to pay 100% of the cost of care, that's fine, and we can design your plan that way. Some clients though, if given the choice, are content with paying a portion of the costs, knowing that it brings the premium down by doing that."

I am telling you, you gain much credibility by taking your time and doing this right. Even if they want XYZ Insurance Company to cover all the expenses, you have shown them that you're looking out for their dollars and that means a lot to them. In this case, Mr. and Mrs. Jones decided they could put $1000 a month toward their care. With the cost of care in their area being $170 per day, we decided on a daily benefit of $140.

As I told Mr. and Mrs. Jones, I believe in using the nursing home costs in their area as the daily benefit indicator. Some clients though, know that they will be relocating to a certain area of the country upon retirement, so it's important for you the agent to know the general costs of care around the United States. Sometimes you will get into a home and the client says they need a certain dollar amount per day, and they are not interested in any input at all. Most of the time though, we have the opportunity to bring our experience to the table. What ever amount is chosen as the daily benefit, write it down in front of them. Remember, it is important to have a rhyme and reason as to the daily benefit amount chosen.

My goal here is to get you the agent to understand *why* you are choosing a certain daily benefit as well as other options that make up a LTC policy. When designing a plan, you must not make it look complicated. You're attitude should seem to say, "No big deal, we do this all the time." If you can speak nonchalantly about the costs of care as an expert, you will put them at ease and help build your credibility. Now we're ready for the next area, the Elimination Period.

Elimination Period

- "Mr. and Mrs. Jones the next part of your plan is the Elimination Period. This is the number of days that you will pay for your care before your benefits in the policy start. Of course, the greater your elimination period, the lower the cost of your policy. The XYZ long term care policy gives you three choices; you can pay for the first 100 days of care, the first 45 days, or the first 20 days. How many days would you feel comfortable paying for out of your own pocket before your policy benefits begin?"

Again, there are choices to be made and there is no one right answer here, just opinions. If the client has considerable assets, then I believe a bigger elimination is fine. Some companies offer a six month or a one year elimination period which is perfect for the individual who has plenty of assets and is willing to take the risk.

My general rule of thumb is, the less they have in assets, the lower the elimination period should be. If you've got a little old lady with a $200,000 farm and only $20,000 in liquid assets, it may not be best for her to go with a 100 day period. You don't want her to have to sell hard assets in order to pay her elimination period.

However, the main goal is the protection of the principle amount of your client's life savings. If someone really needs coverage and affordability is an issue, the 100 day elimination period may be the only way they can fit this plan into their budget. Just make sure they understand how long they have to cover the long term care expenses before their benefits begin. Again, make darned sure they know they're going to have to come up with the money to cover the elimination period.

Do not tell your clients that Medicare will pay for the first 100 days. Read The Guide to Medicare (as you should already have done) if you don't know why. If Mr. Jones replies with something like, "How can I know which elimination period to take until I see some figures?" then respond in this manner:

- "Not a problem Mr. Jones, we can look at all of these elimination periods, but for the sake of discussion, if you were going to pick an elimination period, what does your gut tell you, 100 day, 45 day, or 20 day?"

The reason I give that kind of response is that I don't want a zillion figures written down for them to look at. This just adds more confusion rather than direction. I want to maintain control and help guide them. Their gut feeling will be based on their family experience of needing long term care, and their knowledge of their financial situation.

Once we have chosen all the variables and a price is calculated, then we can make adjustments if needed. The more facts and figures there are to look at, the more Mr. and Mrs. Jones are going to have to think about it rather than make a decision today. Once you have the Elimination Period chosen, write it down on the pad in front of them and continue building their plan.

The Lifetime Maximum Benefit

Once again choices, and once again we're looking for a gut feeling from Mr. and Mrs. Jones. If we can get a response as to what feels right for them, we can determine their level of need. ◊ My experience has taught me that people will select the lifetime maximum benefit based on their family or friends long term care history. ◊ It's really quite amazing. I don't care what statistical information you show them, more often than not, they look at what family or friends went through. The longer the nursing home stay, the more catastrophic it was, the more coverage they want. As I've already stated, your best sales tool is their bad experience. This does not mean that you go for broke when designing a plan. It means you use the "tool" as a means of helping them avoid their own financial devastation if they ever need long term care.

- "Mr. and Mrs. Jones, the next area of the plan is how many years you want XYZ Insurance Company to pay for your care if,

God forbid you would ever need care? The way it works, XYZ Insurance Company allows you to choose a pool of money for your care. The pool can be a set dollar amount all the way up to an unlimited pool of money. The greater the pool of money you choose, the more expensive the plan."

- "The way they help you decide is that they give you four multipliers, 730 days (or two years), 1095 days (three years), 1460 days (four years), or unlimited days (lifetime). It's real simple; we take the daily benefit you've selected, which in this case is $140, and take it times one of the four multipliers. For example: if we took $140, your daily benefit, times 1460 days, four years, that would give you a personal pool of money to pay for your care worth $204,400 now. Remember though, that this amount will compound each year at 5% because of the inflation protection. In ten years, your daily benefit will have grown to $228 per day and your pool of money will be $332,880. Along with your income that you felt you could use to coinsure, it would cover your long term care expenses for four years. Based on your gut and personal history, how long would you want XYZ Insurance Company to pay for your care; two, three, four years, or unlimited years?"

Now again they may say they want to see the difference in the costs, try though, to get some gut reaction as a starting point. Some people say they want nothing but unlimited, or they go to the other end of the spectrum and say that two years is plenty. I usually try to give them two options to look at, that way there isn't just one final cost figure staring at them from the pad of paper. If they want lifetime, I also give them four years. If they say two years, I give them three years as well.

Another reason is this. Many times when they say lifetime only, I know from the financial information I collected that they may not be able to afford a lifetime plan, and I feel that I better kind of settle them down to reality with a lesser option. On the other hand, they may say two years and I know they can afford a much greater plan because of their assets, so I give them another option to consider. Or you can simply do this to get another option on the table. They may say four years and I'll say something like, "Let's look at the four year plan, but for fun let me show you what a lifetime option would run."

Once you get their gut choice, give them one more option with it for them to choose from. Now you have everything you need. Take a few minutes and calculate the plans. Once you have the costs of both plans written down, turn your pad around for them to see. Lay your pen down, and look, listen, and shut up for a minute. At that point they will probably be looking at each other and hopefully saying, "What do you think?" at which point all you do is listen.

If they say nothing and there's silence, you may have scared them by the figures and they might say,

"Well, we have to think about this. We never make quick decisions." If that's the case, more than likely you missed something and moved too quickly early on in the sales process. If you got their approval to go ahead throughout the sales process, you shouldn't be surprised at the end. For the moment, let's assume you did everything right and they are looking at each other as to which option to choose. Proceed with this while holding your pen at the prices on the pad.

- "Which option do you feel is best suited for you? The four year or the lifetime?"
If they are not sure then say this...

- "Mr. and Mrs. Jones, if you are not sure which one is best, may I make a recommendation? If you're not sure, apply for the greater option. If you feel down the road that the four year plan was better suited for you, then you can back it down at any time you please. If you choose the four year option and then down the road want to go for the lifetime, you will then have to health qualify again for the increase. If there is a drastic change in your health between now and then, you may not be able to increase the plan. It's always best to apply for the greater and then back down to the lesser if you're not sure. Does that make sense?"
Usually that does make sense and they choose the greater option at which point you're ready to write it up.

When they give you an affirmative answer, look down at the application and start filling in information. At this point reply with;

- "Great...I'll need the name of your doctor, his address, and phone number."

At this point they will either get up and get that information for you or bring up an objection. Keep writing until an objection is brought up. If they object, put the pen down, relax, and listen to the objection carefully. Then reply and move on. You must be assumptive as discussed in the objection chapter.

Now let's take the other scenario, the silent treatment after you show them the cost of the plans. This is where you suspect sticker shock.

- "Mr. and Mrs. Jones which one these options makes the most sense to you?"

At which point they will probably say something like, "Well we're not sure, we really need to think this over."

- "Ok, I understand. Do you feel looking at the options here that these are within your price range?"

If sticker shock was the issue, you will hear, "This is really more than we were thinking about spending." This might seem like bad news but it really isn't. It's late in the game, but you're finally going to be pointed in the right direction.

- "How much were you thinking it might cost?"

To which you will probably hear, "We really didn't know. That's why we had you in. We really just wanted some idea and didn't expect to do anything today." At this point you need to get the "sticker shock prices" off the table. If the earlier parts of the interview were done properly, you know the long term care experiences they have seen, and that they are concerned it may happen to them. They may have really been hoping that LTC insurance was an option for them to protect themselves, but the cost of the insurance scared them.

- "I understand, and that's why I'm here, to help you get the options you need in order to make a decision. Let's take a look at the two year option and see what you think. The main thing today is not to lock you into something, but to see if this is affordable and then to make sure you can qualify for coverage. Even if you told me today that you wanted coverage I can't guarantee that you would qualify. So let's take a look at the two year plan."

At this point get out a <u>new</u> sheet of paper and get the higher priced options out of the way. Figure the less expensive option for them. Build up that option in a positive way, emphasizing that having some coverage for long term care is better than no coverage at all.

- "How does this look? Is this better suited for you?"

If you are now in the ballpark they will say, "Well its better, but I still think we need to think this over."

- "Great, but you feel this might be affordable?"

If you hear, "Maybe, probably." then you may be on your way to writing up an application.

- "Great! Mr. and Mrs. Jones, if you feel this might be affordable may I make a recommendation? As I mentioned earlier, my two main goals here today were to design an affordable plan for you, one that would not change your standard of living. If we could do that, to then see if XYZ Insurance Company would approve both of you for coverage. If you feel this might be affordable, let's go ahead and get the name of your doctor, his address and phone number. Let's submit an application and get you both through the underwriting process. What is your doctor's name?"

Begin to write on the application again with your head looking down expecting them to get up and get the information you requested. If they get up, ask them to bring you any medications that they are taking so you can get a look at the dosages. I know this seems simplistic but it works. We've all heard the term closer. Well a closer is nothing more than a salesman who moves forward in an assumptive way, always believing he's getting the check. ◊ There are no magic phrases that make a sale, just confident salesmen asking for the check. ◊ If you have prepared the client properly early on describing how a LTC policy is approved, you won't have to ask for the check, they'll get up from the table and grab their checkbook.

Extras

Just a word about adding extras to a policy. The Daily Benefit, Elimination Period, and Lifetime Maximum are the main ingredients of a long term care policy. This is the reason you are there. I remember years ago being in a potential clients home where I was in a competitive situation with another company. I was comparing apples to apples as far as the coverage was concerned, believing that the superiority of my company would make up for any difference in price with this other company. Well, the thing I remember about this particular appointment was that the policy offered by the competition had an ambulance benefit and the client had really taken note of that. In fact he did not take out my policy because of that simple extra benefit.

Now I had only been in the business a short time, and I'm sure I didn't do the best with this gentleman, but I was incredulous that he couldn't see that you don't make a decision about your LTC policy based on some stupid ambulance benefit. Looking back, I see that there were some good lessons here. First, what "you" think is most important doesn't always win out, and second, give the customer what he or she wants.

Extras are not the main reason you're there, but sometimes they can make or break a sale for you. I wish I had had some of the extras available when I started in the business years ago. Creative payment options for one, and the return of premium option. The return of premium I especially like and believe it would have really added to my business. Extras like that can really help solidify the sale and keep that policy from being replaced and the renewal commissions flowing. So keep this in mind when you're in the home. Stick to the basics and do a good job, but don't forget that extras can sometimes make the difference.

9. Fill out the application, paperwork, and collect the check. You're almost home, just a little bit longer. By now you've agreed on a plan and price. Hopefully they're going for their doctor's information as well as the check book. You're in good shape but don't count your money yet, there is still work to be done. If you need something to sober you at this point, take into consideration that once you collect all the information and turn it in to the insurer, they could still be declined or your clients could cancel the process before it's completed. Yuck! So remember, take it slow and easy. Cross every t and dot every i. I can tell you from first hand experience that nothing is more depressing than to screw up on the application and have to go back to the client to correct something or get another signature that you forgot.

Take everything page by page. Be incredibly organized, and write legibly. If the insurance company underwriters have to guess at what you've written, I can promise that it won't go well for you. In the case of filling out the application, concise accurate information is best. You need to be as concise as possible but substantial enough to get the job done. These underwriters have one heck of a job to do, and you need to provide the tools for them to do it. Developing good relationships with the underwriters involves submitting well written accurate applications.

- Go into the appointment with an application pack already organized and ready to go. You don't want to look unprofessional by not having all the forms with you.
- Make sure you get the doctors name, address, phone number, and the last time they saw their doctor. Also, don't forget to write in the reason why they went to the doctor.
- List the names and doses of medications they are taking. Include how long they have been taking them and the reason.
- Make sure that the age they give you lines up with their birth date.

I can't tell you how many times people have told me they were a certain age, but when I figured their age by their birth date it showed them to be older or younger than they said. Early in my career I sold a policy to a lady who had told me she was 64 years old. I believed her without checking it against the actual birth date. When I got back to the office, the main computer wouldn't accept her information and pricing I had computed. It turned out the woman was actually 67. When I called her with hopes of taking care of it, she was so upset that she cancelled the application. I have never forgotten that valuable lesson. It probably would have been a different story if I had dealt with it in the home.

- Check the premium calculations several times before leaving the home, or better yet, use a laptop computer with company software to avoid mistakes.
- Check, check, and recheck for signatures before you leave.
- When you get back to the office, be sure to make copies of everything, including the check.

10. Go through the brochure. Once you've completed the application process you're ready for the brochure. I know that many of you were wondering if I would ever get to that. Well, you need to know something very important that could put you light years ahead in this business. Here is a truth:

◊ The brochure itself doesn't sell anything and the sooner you learn that the better off you'll be. Only a pencil pusher or someone who knows nothing about *how to sell* believes that a brochure is to be used as a sales tool. ◊

Now don't misunderstand, I believe you need to have that brochure in YOUR BONES. This is a truth; my experience has shown me that most of the top, agents rarely use the brochure in the sales process. The reason? They have it inside of them and it shows. You need to know everything about what you're selling and in time you will, but selling is about communication, not reading a book together. That's why I have all the paperwork filled out and ready to go before I crack open "The Brochure." The brochure is used to solidify the sale, not make the sale. What I like to do is just hit the high points of their plan, making notes all over the place. Use a high lighter and lot's of underlining too. Don't be slack here. Be methodical and very neat with your notes and highlighting. Act like you know your stuff, as you should.

11. Get referrals. When done, put a nice packet of information together for them along with several of your business cards for friends and neighbors. People love trinkets too. Leave them something like a calendar or a magnet with your name and number on it, and ink pens. People love ink pens. I used to use a certain brand of pen for many years. I had many complements on those pens and gave many away. You want to give these people every reason not to cancel and when you give stuff out it tends to obligate them a bit. Buyers remorse is a very real thing, and the first few days after the sale can sometimes cause people to have a whole new attitude about writing that $5000 check. Anything you can do to help solidify the sale is good.

The way to win these days in the long term care business is through referrals. The number of weekly appointments you set will determine the success you have, it's all numbers. Agents are constantly striving for ways to increase their number of appointments through all kinds of creative thinking. Sometimes though, the answer is right before them and that answer is referrals. The agents out there that have established themselves as honest ethical people in their area seem to benefit more than the average agent as far as getting referrals. The reason is they are established and known, you can do the same.

One company that I have dealt with in the Midwest started in the senior market in 1990 with two people and has now grown to twelve full time employees. Part of the reason for their growth was through referrals, word of mouth, and other creative ways. The owner explained, "Whenever I had an appointment, I would always visit the neighbors and introduce myself." That one little idea helped grow his company to where it is today.

So when you're with these people, be thinking ahead and realize that the more referrals you get, the less your cost for leads and the greater your profit. Leads and seminars are effective, but can also be a burden financially. Referrals just make sense. So once you have finished with all the paper work and are ready to leave, sit back one more minute and ask a few more questions.

- "Mr. and Mrs. Jones do you feel that this has been a good experience for the both of you?"
- "Do you feel you know more now about the issue of long term care than you did yesterday?"
- "I wonder if you feel this information would be of value to any of your friends or family. Can you give me two names of

people you know, which know and respect you?"

- "Do either of you belong to a group or organization that invites speakers to come in and talk about a certain subject? Would you be willing to put me in touch with the individuals that are in charge of bringing people in to speak to these groups?"

Remember what the close is? Just be willing to ask the question and do it consistently and you will reap the benefits. Don't expect anything if you're not willing to ask for it. Persevere and the truth about numbers will work in your favor. The fruit is on the tree just waiting for you the agent to pick it. A few solid years in this business working consistently for referrals will reap rewards for years to come.

12. Leave information and make delivery arrangements. Everything you do at the appointment is important. From the moment you get out of the car to the delivery arrangements for their policies. This is where you are giving final instructions on what will be taking place over the next four to six weeks. Since it is such a long period of time, it's very important for you to give them a map of coming events as well as encouraging them in their decision to purchase long term care insurance.

This is a major decision for them, one they have usually thought about for some time. There is a lot of emotion involved in this decision, and buyers remorse can rear its ugly head and spoil the whole deal if you leave these people without closing all the doors properly. Take out a piece of paper, and as you describe the process to come, draw out a timeline for them to refer back to. This is how I explain it.

- "Mr. and Mrs. Jones let me again show you how the process works. Your application is sent to the XYZ Insurance Company. Within the next couple of weeks, you should be getting a call from the company to verify the information given on the application. They may also want to ask you a few health questions if they feel they need to gather more information. Sometimes they may also send someone out to take a look at you to make sure you can walk and talk. (*That usually gets a laugh.*) Many times the questions they ask seem silly, but they really do have a method behind them. They just want to make sure that you are not ready for a nursing home now. You both will do great and I'm sure you will not have a problem. I just feel that it's important to prepare you so you know what to expect. It's an extremely simple process and the XYZ Insurance Company is very good at it."
- "In four to six weeks when the policy is issued, I will call you and make arrangements for its delivery. In the meantime, if you have any questions, feel free to call me or make a note of the

question on the brochure and we can cover
it when I deliver the policy. Okay? Any
further questions?"

Now you are almost done, but one big hurdle
remains. Pause, look them in the eye soberly and say:

- "Mr. and Mrs. Jones, we covered a lot of
territory today. We've talked about some
things that are not very pleasant, and we've
taken steps to help protect the principle
amount of your life savings. My question
to both of you is, how do you feel about
taking out an XYZ policy today?"

SHUT UP AND LISTEN

It's at this point, with their words and actions, that
you find out how good of a job you've done, and if they
are on the road to truly being sold. Remember, they
are not fully and completely sold until their policies
are in hand and it is past the 30 day free look period.
Truthfully, it's not until they are in their second year of
paying for their policy.

What they say with their body language will speak
volumes. Once they share their feelings, then you can
address any concerns or doubts they may have, and if
necessary pull out the brochure and clarify where there
might be confusion or any misunderstanding.

◊ It is important for Mr. and Mrs. Jones to verbalize
why they are doing this today. ◊ Have you ever had to tell
someone in your family why you needed to do something
difficult but necessary? Any parent can probably give

you many instances of having to do the right, but very hard thing, when dealing with their children. My wife and I have always found that when we were together on something we were an unstoppable team. In the same way, Mr. and Mrs. Jones need to not only agree together, but they need to be able to communicate and verbalize their agreement too. This will help them begin to have the assurance and confidence that they have truly made a wise decision. You need to ask them at least one of these questions.

- "Mr. and Mrs. Jones do you feel more at peace knowing we've taken steps here today to protect the principle amount of your life savings?"
- "Mr. and Mrs. Jones what do you think your children will say about your decision to take out a long term care policy?"
- "Mr. and Mrs. Jones, I've found that many children believe they can take care of their parents should they ever need long term care. What do your children think?"

Again, get them to tell you why. Leave no stone unturned. Ask questions and commend them for taking action. Make yourself available in case their children have any questions. The truth is people will do what they want and don't really need their children's approval, but some families have situations where the kids almost take over. ◊ If you detect that the kids make the decisions when you're either on the phone or when you arrive in the home, <u>reschedule for a time when the kids can be there</u>. ◊

Through the years I've learned the hard way and have had many disappointments when it came to the kids. Involve them if need be. Not sure, but I think there's been only a few times since 1989 that I ever lost a sale when the kids were present. Once the kids understand what long term care really means, they are all for a policy that can not only pay for care, but also protect their inheritance.

The big finish.

Well you've made it through and have an application in hand, you're done. . .for now. It's time to thank them and to see if your sale can stand the test of time. You will win some and lose some, that's a part of life for the long term care salesman. The highs are high, and the lows are low. Know this though, if you work hard and can get a few years under your belt, you'll never be the same. You will never be willing to punch a clock again.

Concerning the delivery of the policy, there are many schools of thought on how it should be done. You want to do what you're most comfortable with. I always like to deliver it in person. Others would call their clients as soon as the policy came in, congratulate them on their approval, and let them know it was coming in the mail. Use what ever works best for you. One idea though, when you deliver it in person you get another chance to cement the deal by dealing with any buyers remorse you detect, and to collect more referrals.

There is much more that I could have shared, but some things you are going to have to find out for yourself. Now pick up the phone and get busy making money!

CHAPTER 9

Gems of Truth

◊ Product knowledge is important, but don't be overly concerned feeling that you have to know everything about the long term care policy you are selling in order to be an effective salesman. ◊ Ch 1

◊ When the client has a question about a benefit or a feature and you're not sure what the answer is offhand let the brochure or outline of coverage do the speaking for you. ◊ Ch 1

◊ When you've made a sale, never leave the home before you have checked to make sure that all the paperwork is filled out!! ◊ Ch 1

◊ Even the worst Salesman will be successful if he or she consistently sets appointments, even the worst. ◊ Ch 2

◊ Prepare for your phone time and eliminate distractions. ◊ Ch 2

◊ Your phone call is the first impression your customers have of you. ◊ Ch 2

◊ It is important to <u>not</u> take a defensive approach when making calls, but to remain calm and relaxed. ◊ Ch 2

◊ An objection does not require a *detailed* response, but a *simple answer* and a continuation of the appointment setting process. ◊ Ch 4

◊ Let your response be determined by listening closely, then speaking. ◊ Ch 4

◊ The more real and natural you are on the phone, the less you will have to deal with objections. ◊ Ch 4

◊ No matter what the objection, you just keep plowing ahead. ◊ Ch 4

◊ Never burn a bridge unless you absolutely have to.◊ Ch 4

◊ There are many things that are out of your control…don't sweat those. The things that are in your control. . . change those for the better. ◊ Ch 5

◊ I want a relationship, but I also want to have a sale. I'm going to make lots of friends, but I want to make a living. ◊ Ch 7

◊ You do not want to memorize what to say. You want to work on how you express yourself to Mr. and Mrs. Jones. ◊ Ch 7

◊ Let your gut be your guide, it does not lie. ◊ Ch 8

◊ You the Agent decide what the client is going to buy. The good agent, however, makes them think they are the ones making all the decisions. ◊ Ch 8

◊ The number one problem we face today is the health situation of the client and being able to place the clients business, not the cost of the insurance as some so called experts say. ◊ Ch 8

◊ Do a lot of writing with each health condition they mention, nodding as you go. Do a lot of hmmm sounds keeping a serious expression on your face. ◊ Ch 8

◊ We have a responsibility to speak the truth in love. That sometimes calls for a *teensy* bit of pain, but never to be rude or offensive. ◊ Ch 8

◊ It has been said that, "We as agents must create need." to which I say no, "We expose the need that is already there." ◊ Ch 8

◊ The best sales tool we have is their bad experience. You are looking for a bad experience. ◊ Ch 8

◊ The Mr. and Mrs. Joneses of the world respect a take charge person if they feel they are being directed under consent. ◊ Ch 8

◊ The bottom line is that this long term care insurance business is all about money; the client's money and their family's inheritance. ◊ Ch 8

◊ It's important for you to know why you as the agent sold a particular plan and to be able to explain yourself with some logic attached. ◊ Ch 8

◊ When designing plans and comparing options, use a lap top computer complete with software provided by the companies that sell LTC insurance. ◊ Ch 8

◊ Coinsuring, if done correctly, is a wonderful option for many people. ◊ Ch 8

◊ My experience has taught me that people will select the lifetime maximum benefit based on their family or friends long term care history. ◊ Ch 8

◊ There are no magic phrases that make a sale, just confident salesmen asking for the check. ◊ Ch 8

◊ The brochure itself doesn't sell anything and the sooner you learn that the better off you'll be. Only a pencil pusher or someone who knows nothing about *how to sell* believes that a brochure is to be used as a sales tool. ◊ Ch 8

◊ It is important for Mr. and Mrs. Jones to verbalize why they are doing this today. ◊ Ch 8

◊ If you detect that the kids make the decisions when you're either on the phone or when you arrive in the home, <u>reschedule for a time when the kids can be there</u>. ◊ Ch 8

CHAPTER 10

Helpful sources

As an agent, it's always nice to have some resources at your fingertips. Here are a few:

This is a good source for every LTC Agent wanting to excel in their understanding of long term care issues. The CLTC designation shows your professional commitment.

- Corporation for Long-Term Care Certification, Inc. www.ltc-cltc.com or you can contact their National Marketing Office at 114 Williams Street, Lancaster, SC 29720. Their toll free number is 866-383-2075.

Here is a high quality lead provider for long term care agents.

- Online Insurance Services, LLC found at www.USIMC.org Agents can register and then check out the site, or you can

preview it first by typing in 'guest1' as the
username and password. (To order leads
you will have to be registered.)

Long term care information resource covering just
about anything you could think of.

- LTC Connection www.ltcconnection.com
  or write them at 6755 Earl Drive #100,
  Colorado Springs, CO 80918. You can call
  them at (719) 522-0596, Ext. 205

A couple of resources for all kinds of sales and
marketing tools.

- American Association for Long-Term Care
  Insurance www.AALTCI.org or call them
  at (818) 597-3227. They offer free audios
  with sales and marketing tips.
- Sales Creators www.LTCSales.com or call
  (888) 599-5997. They publish the LTCi
  Sales Strategies magazine and organize the
  annual National LTCi Producers Summit.

A source for contracting with LTC companies as
well as support for every aspect of the LTC insurance
process from quoting to delivering the policy.

- LTC Compass www.LTCCompass.com
  or write them at One Lakeside Commons,

990 Hammond Drive, Suite 200, Atlanta,
GA 30328 Their phone number is (770)
394-3800.

CHAPTER 11

One More tool

This guide has been about equipping the long term care insurance agent with the tools necessary to get the job done. One more tool to add icing on the cake involves a company that I'm extremely passionate about; Oak Street Funding. In April 2004, I was asked to join them as their Field Sales Manager. In Oak Street Funding I saw an opportunity for insurance agents that had never been offered before.

One of the biggest problems that established agents face is their ability to get the capital they need to grow their business. Their source has always been the local bank or credit cards, which either limits the dollars available or ties up personal assets which many, rightly so, are against. Think about it, are you willing to put your personal wealth, your home, or other property up as the collateral source?

In the past, those were the only options, and not very good ones. The insurance business is ever changing and requires investment if you want to grow your business. Have you ever had the opportunity to purchase another agents book of business or an agency but were unable to come up with the cash needed? Where was your local bank? How about the property and casualty agent that puts hundreds of thousands if not millions of dollars through their local bank, yet the bank is unwilling to loan the funds needed?

This is the problem faced by many agents. Did you know that your book of business, those wonderful renewal commissions, is not considered an asset by the bank? That day is over and maybe the answer to what you've been searching for is here.

Let me share what possibilities exist with Oak Street Funding. Simply put, Oak Street Funding is a commercial finance company that loans insurance agents money based on their renewal commissions. Whatever your renewals are paying you, Oak Street Funding can loan 2-3 times that amount.

For example, let's say you've got a long term care book of business that's paying $100,000 in renewal commissions. Oak Street Funding can loan you $200,000 to $300,000! Here's the real kicker. The loan is collateralized by your book/agency, not your personal assets, not hard assets, not the money you have set aside.

Oak Street Funding offers the average agent, as well as the big time producers and brokerage companies access to some serious capital. The standard loan size ranges from $20,000 to $2.5 million. For the company that needs much more, we can help there too.

What I have just told you can change the way you think about doing business forever. Finally, somebody recognizes the value of a book of business. To the insurance agent, this is nothing new; we've always known what a truly valuable asset this is.

Now if you think that was good, I've got one more bit of icing to tell you about and this is guaranteed to blow you away. I told you how Oak Street Funding can loan 2-3 times your renewals. Let's say for instance, you find an agency for sale and you want to buy it. The agency is producing $1 million in commission per year and the asking price is $2.1 million.

You go to your local bank for a loan and they say, "Sure, no problem. What do you have for collateral?" You say that you have a few thousand dollars in the bank and a house with a mortgage. Nothing else, but that you wanted to use the renewal commissions from the agency that you are buying as the collateral source. You know the answer, "No way!" In the past that thought of buying an agency and growing your business would have ended then and there. Until now.

That's right; Oak Street Funding will use the commissions from the agency or book that *you want to buy* as the collateral source for the loan. Now stop and realize what I just told you. You can buy books or agencies all day long, never having to use your own assets. You now have the ability to grow your business like never before. Give Oak Street Funding a call today. We're ready to help you grow. 866-Oak-Fund.

About the Author

After 15 years as an insurance agent in the LTC business, Curt Vahle presently works as the Field Sales Manager for Oak Street Funding; a company dedicated to assisting insurance agents with their capital needs. He also works as a speaker and teacher for agents, agencies, and insurance companies desiring to grow their LTC business with a "real world" approach to selling. Curt and his wife Judy have four grown children, one grandchild (so far), and he is an absolute acoustic guitar fanatic.

To bring Curt into your company or organization as a speaker, or for an in depth sales training course, feel free to call and leave a message at (317) 690-8614. You may also write him at ltccurt@yahoo.com ; Curt welcomes all correspondences.

LaVergne, TN USA
24 October 2010
202067LV00001B/85/A